Library

 community services

 North Lanarkshire Council

HOW THE BRAIN WORKS

LIZ GOGERLY

Adapted from an original text by Carol Ballard

W

FRANKLIN WATTS
LONDON·SYDNEY

First published in 2009 by Franklin Watts

Copyright © 2009 Arcturus Publishing Limited

Franklin Watts
338 Euston Road
London NW1 3BH

Franklin Watts Australia
Level 17/207 Kent Street, Sydney, NSW 2000

Produced by Arcturus Publishing Limited,
26/27 Bickels Yard, 151–153 Bermondsey Street, London SE1 3HA

Understanding the Human Body is based on the series *Exploring the Human Body*, published by Franklin Watts.

Editor: Alex Woolf
Designer: Peta Phipps and Mike Reynolds
Illustrator: Michael Courtney
Picture researcher: Glass Onion Pictures
Consultant: Dr Kristina Routh

Picture Credits
Science Photo Library: 4 (TEK Image), 6 (Alfred Pasieka), 9 (Colin Cuthbert), 11 (Sheila Terry), 15 (BSIP, Barouillet), 18 (Renée Lynn), 21 (Martin Riedl), 22 (Sheila Terry), 24 (Oscar Burriel), 26 (Oscar Burriel), 29 (David Constantine).
Topfoto: 16 (Ellen Senisi / The Image Works).
Shutterstock: cover (Laurence Gough).

A CIP catalogue record for this book is available from the British Library.

Dewey Decimal Classification Number: 612.8'2

ISBN 978 0 7496 9054 0

Printed in China

Franklin Watts is a is a division of Hachette Children's Books, an Hachette UK Company
www.hachette.co.uk

Contents

What are the **Brain** and **Nerves?**

Your brain controls everything in your body. Even when you are fast asleep the brain is working. It keeps your heart beating and controls your breathing.

Movement

Every move you make is possible because of your brain. It controls all the muscles in your body. The brain allows you to run and jump. It even lets you wiggle your toes.

Thoughts and feelings

Your brain allows you to think and learn. It's where all your dreams and ideas are made. Every feeling and emotion you have is possible because of your brain.

The nervous system

The brain is connected to every part of your body by **nerves**. The nerves carry messages to and from the brain. Organs such as your eyes pick up information from the world around you. The nerves send this information to the brain.

Your brain allows you to remember information.

The spinal cord

In your back there is a long, thin bundle of nerves. This is called the **spinal cord**. It connects the brain to your nervous system. It's the most important connection to the brain. If your spinal cord is damaged, you may not be able to move or think properly. The spinal cord is protected by your backbone, or **spine**.

This diagram shows the brain and nervous system in the human body.

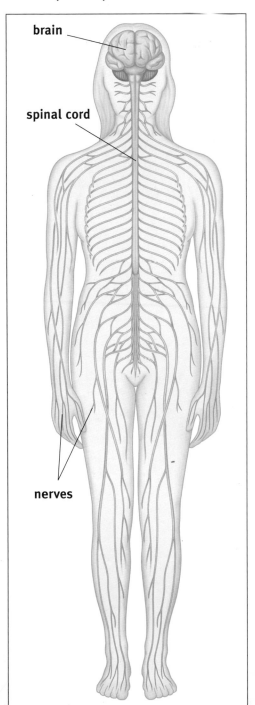

brain

spinal cord

nerves

○
Q&A

Why should I wear a safety helmet?

The brain is very delicate. If it is damaged, your body may not work properly. The **skull** is made of thick bone. It protects your brain. But a hard knock could still break the skull and harm your brain. A safety helmet gives extra protection for your brain. People usually wear helmets for sports such as cricket, horse riding, skateboarding and cycling.

Inside the Brain

Your brain is about the size of a small cauliflower. It is pinkish-grey and looks wrinkled. An adult's brain weighs about 1,300 to 1,400 grams. It contains more than 100,000,000,000 (one hundred thousand million) **nerve cells**!

Protecting the brain

The brain is wrapped inside three thin layers called meninges. Between the brain and meninges there is a liquid called cerebrospinal fluid. This liquid stops the brain banging against the bones in the **skull**.

Parts of the brain

The brain has four main parts. These are called the cerebrum, **cerebellum**, diencephalon and brainstem. Each part has its own special job to do.

The cerebrum

The cerebrum makes up nearly nine-tenths of the brain. We use the cerebrum to think. It has two halves called the left and right cerebral hemispheres.

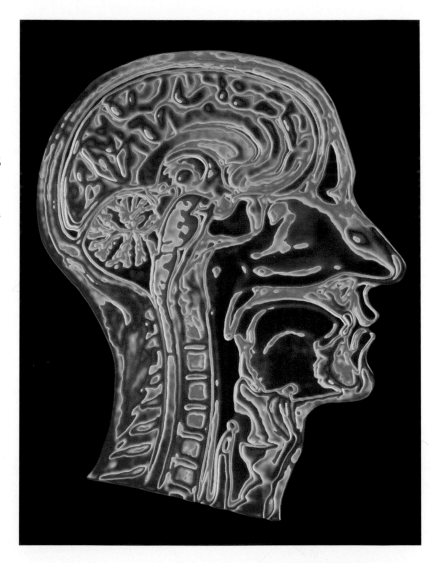

A modern hospital scanner was used to take this image of the brain.

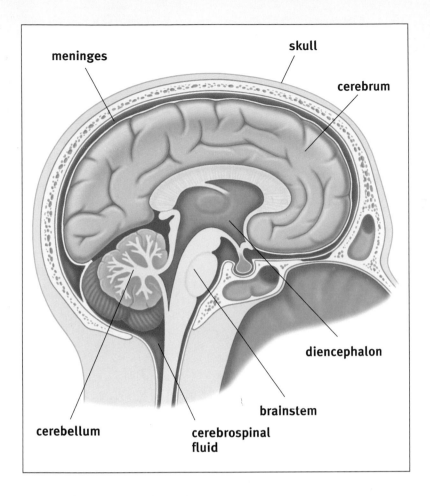

meninges

skull

cerebrum

diencephalon

brainstem

cerebellum

cerebrospinal
fluid

This diagram shows the main parts of the brain.

The cerebellum

The cerebellum makes up about one-tenth of the brain. It helps us to keep our balance and stand straight. It allows us to make smooth movements.

The diencephalon

The diencephalon is the centre of the brain. It helps to control how we feel. The diencephalon also connects to our senses. For example, it allows us to know when we are hungry or thirsty.

The brainstem

The brainstem connects to the **spinal cord**. It controls everything you need in order to stay alive, including breathing, digestion and the beating of your heart.

Q&A

How does blood get to the brain?

The brain needs blood to work. Blood supplies oxygen and **nutrients**. It also removes waste products. Two **arteries** take blood from the heart to the upper and front parts of the brain. Two other arteries supply the back of the brain. Blood is carried around the brain through a network of smaller **blood vessels**.

Map of the Brain

The outer layer of your brain is called the **cerebral cortex**. The surface of the cerebral cortex has lots of bumps and grooves. It looks rather like a walnut!

This diagram shows the jobs carried out in different parts of the brain.

Areas of the cerebral cortex

Sensory areas are for receiving signals from the rest of the body.

Motor areas are for sending signals to the rest of the body.

Association areas are for making sense of the information coming into the brain. They also decide what your body needs to do.

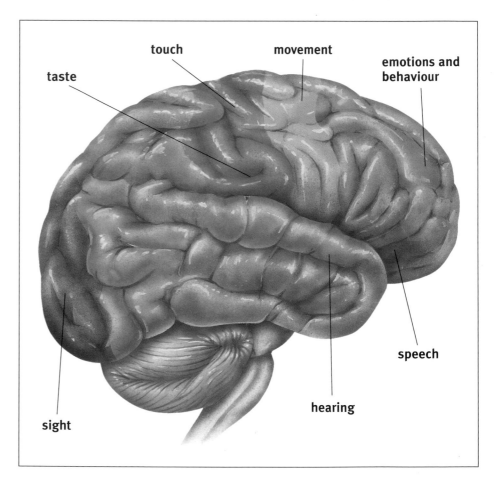

taste

touch

movement

emotions and behaviour

sight

hearing

speech

Emotions, speech and movement

The front of the cerebral cortex controls your emotions. Motor areas in the front part of the brain allow you to speak. They also control many of your movements.

This therapist (right) is helping a stroke patient learn to speak again.

Taste and touch

The top of the cerebral cortex controls your senses of taste and touch. The sensory areas here receive signals from your skin, muscles, joints and body organs. This information is sorted out, then passed on to other parts of the brain for action to be taken.

Hearing, sight and smell

The sides of the cerebral cortex control your sense of hearing. They also allow you to keep your balance. The back of the cerebral cortex controls your sense of sight. The centre of the cerebral cortex allows you to smell.

Q&A

What happens when someone has a 'stroke'?

A stroke is also called a 'brain attack'. A stroke happens when the blood supply to the brain is stopped. The brain needs a supply of blood at all times. When the blood is cut off, some parts of the brain can be damaged. This damage may mean a person cannot move or speak properly again. Some patients recover from strokes.

Left Brain, Right Brain

The cerebrum is made up from two parts. These are called the left hemisphere and the right hemisphere. The left hemisphere controls the right side of the body. The right hemisphere controls the left side of the body. The hemispheres work together to let you do anything you like.

The left hemisphere

In most people, the left hemisphere controls speaking, reading and writing. The left hemisphere is working when you are chatting to your friends. It is also working when you are reading a book or doing some maths.

The right hemisphere

In most people, the right hemisphere deals with creative activities. The right hemisphere is working when you are looking at shapes and colours. It's also working when you are painting, drawing or playing a musical instrument.

These pictures show which activities are controlled by each side of the brain.

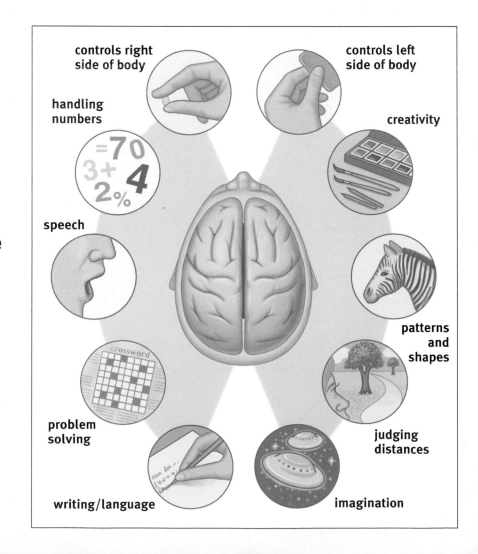

controls right side of body

controls left side of body

handling numbers

creativity

speech

patterns and shapes

problem solving

judging distances

writing/language

imagination

The right hemisphere controls creative activities like painting.

Q&A

What happens if I'm left-handed?

Nine out of ten people are right-handed. One person in ten is left-handed. Left-handed people use their left hand for writing, using scissors or throwing a ball. They may kick with their left foot too! Many creative people are left-handed. Famous left-handed people include Leonardo da Vinci, Beethoven, Paul McCartney, Angelina Jolie and John McEnroe. Some people use both hands equally well. They are said to be ambidextrous.

Baby brains

When you were a baby, each hemisphere worked in the same way. By the time you were eight, one of the hemispheres became stronger. In nine out of ten people, the left hemisphere is stronger.

Some people are better at creative things. Other people may find maths easier. This is because of the way our brains are formed when we are young.

Linking the **Brain** and **Body**

Nerves connect the brain to the body. Nerves are made up from **nerve cells**. Each nerve cell has three main parts.

The **cell** body is the cell's control centre. The fine threads (dendrites) carry signals from other nerve cells to the cell body. The long, thin fibre (the axon) carries signals away from the cell body to other nerve cells.

The tiny gaps between each nerve cell are called synapses. Chemicals called neurotransmitters carry signals across these gaps.

Here you can see the three main parts of a nerve cell.

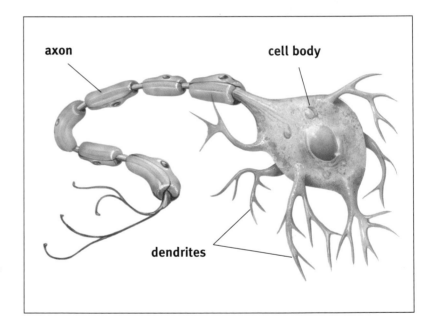

axon

cell body

dendrites

Bundles of nerves

Nerve cells are packed together in bundles. These bundles have a protective layer. The bundles are then arranged to make a larger bundle. An outer layer keeps the bundle together. This is called a nerve. Some nerves are very thick, with thousands of nerve fibres. Other nerves may only have a few nerve fibres.

Cranial nerves

Cranial nerves link the brain to the eyes, ears, nose and tongue. The vagus nerve is the largest cranial nerve. It connects the brain to the heart, lungs, stomach, intestines, liver and kidneys.

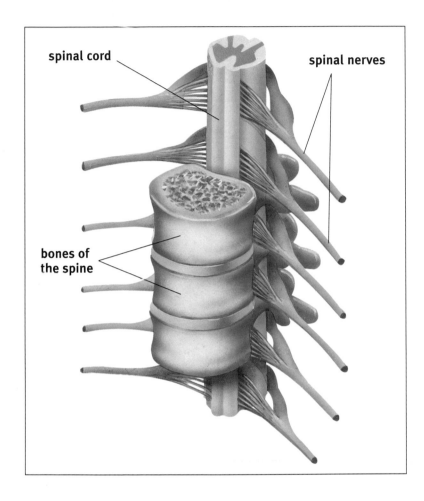

spinal cord

spinal nerves

bones of the spine

This shows how the bones of the spine fit around the spinal cord.

Spinal cord

The **spinal cord** connects the brain to the rest of the body. It is found inside the **spinal canal.** The spinal canal is like a tunnel made by the bones of the **spine.** The top of the spinal cord is joined to the brain at the brainstem.

Q&A

What are reflex reactions?

When you touch something hot, your hand probably jerks away quickly. This is called a **reflex** reaction. The signal that you have touched something hot never reaches the brain. The signal takes a short cut. Your spinal cord sends your hand a message to move instead. This is a way of keeping your body safe in dangerous situations.

Sensing the World

People have five senses – sight, hearing, touch, taste and smell. Each sense has a **sense organ**. This collects information and sends it to the brain. Our eyes gather light information. Our ears collect sound information. **Receptors** in our skin receive information about touch, temperature and pressure. Our tongues and noses collect information about food, drink and the air around us.

The diagram shows how the brain gets information from the eyes.

Electrical signals

When the sense organs have gathered information, they send out an electrical signal. The signal travels along a **nerve** to the brain. The sensory area in the brain picks up this information. The sensory area and association area begin working together. They make sense of the information and act on it.

Sight

Light information from the eyes is sent along the optic nerve. This information travels to the visual centre of the brain. The brain can work out this information. It lets you know what you are seeing.

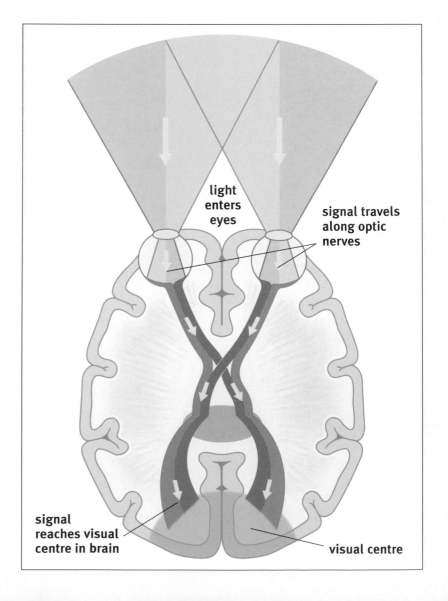

light enters eyes

signal travels along optic nerves

signal reaches visual centre in brain

visual centre

Hearing

Sound information from the ears is sent along the auditory nerve. This information reaches the hearing sensory area of the brain. The brain can work out this information. It lets you know what you are hearing.

Nerve endings in the skin pick up information about the cat's soft fur.

Touch

Receptors in our skin respond to different things. Some respond to touch. Others may pick up information about temperature. The information is sent to the touch sensory area of the brain. The brain then works out what you have felt.

Q&A

How do we taste and smell?

Taste buds in the surface of the tongue pick up information about food and drink. Receptors in the nose pick up chemicals in the air. All this information is sent to the brain. The brain then works out what you have tasted or smelt.

Movement

The brain controls all your movements. You decide when you want to make a movement. Then the motor areas of the **cerebral cortex** send signals to your muscles. These signals are sent along motor **nerves**. The signals cause your muscles to contract and move. Most muscles move bones. Muscles in your face move skin.

Smooth moves

The brain works in other ways to make you move well. Your brain has a system of constant checks. These help you to move smoothly. This system helps you to remember certain ways of moving. A movement becomes easier the more often you do it. This is because the brain remembers the movement. It improves the movement every time you make it.

The cerebellum allows you to learn to play musical instruments.

The cerebellum

The part of the brain called the **cerebellum** is involved in the checking system. The cerebellum also receives information about your movements. When a muscle starts to contract, signals are sent to the cerebellum.

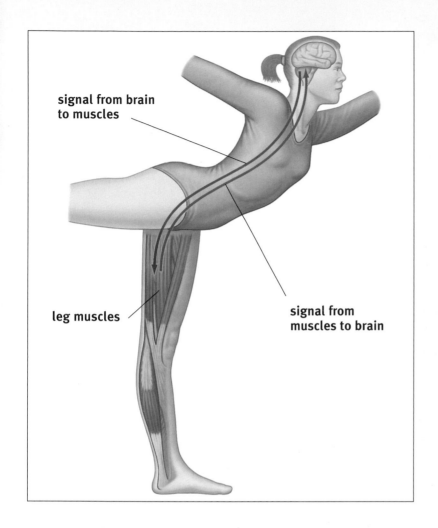

signal from brain
to muscles

leg muscles

signal from
muscles to brain

This diagram shows how
the feedback system works.

Feedback

The information sent back to the cerebellum is called
feedback. The cerebellum then corrects any problems
with the movement. The **cerebral cortex** (the 'thinking'
part of the brain) is not involved in this process.
Therefore, you are able to move without having to
think about it.

Learning to move

The cerebellum helps us to learn new skills all the time.
Learning to dance or play a new sport are possible
because of the cerebellum. Every time you practise the
new skill the cerebellum remembers what to do. The
feedback system means that you get better at it.

Q&A

How do we balance?

Receptors all around the
body send feedback to
the cerebellum. The
cerebellum keeps a check
on the exact position of
every part of your body.
This helps you to keep
your balance.

Controlling your Body

The brain and nervous system keep your body alive. They work together to make sure that everything in your body is working properly. The part of the brain and nervous system that does this is called the **autonomic nervous system** (ANS).

What the ANS does

The ANS keeps your body going without you knowing it. It controls most things that go on in your body. If you are too hot, it works to cool you down. The ANS also controls:

- how fast your heart beats;
- how quickly you breathe in and out;
- the movement of food through your **digestive system**;
- the production of sweat, tears and saliva;
- how much sugar, water and minerals there is in your blood;
- the removal of waste products by your kidneys.

How the ANS works

The ANS has two parts: the sympathetic system and the parasympathetic system. The sympathetic system speeds things up.

The ANS helps your body to cool down after exercise.

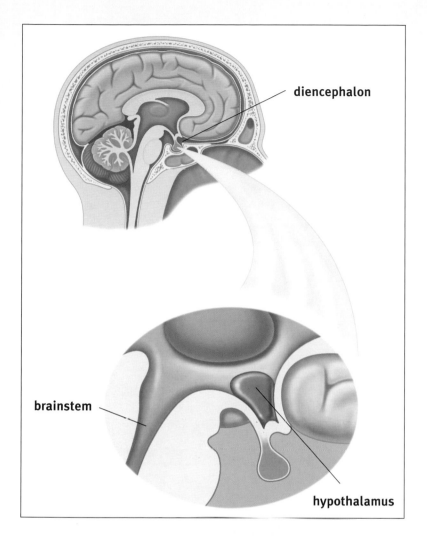

diencephalon

brainstem

hypothalamus

The hypothalamus is part of the diencephalon, deep inside the brain.

When you exercise, the sympathetic system makes your heart beat faster. The parasympathetic system slows things down. When you stop exercising, the parasympathetic system makes your heart slow down.

Most of the time the two systems work together and keep your body in a stable state. Sometimes the balance is upset. Then one system takes over until the body is brought back to its normal state.

Q&A

What is the body clock?

The ANS is mainly controlled by the **hypothalamus**. A small area of the hypothalamus is called the body clock. The body clock has a 24-hour cycle. It maintains your body's daily patterns. These affect when you feel awake or sleepy. When our body clock cycle is upset, we feel tired. Many people have 'jet lag' after a long flight. This is because the body clock has to change its cycle.

Memory and **Learning**

Our brain allows us to learn things and store memories. Doctors and scientists are still trying to find out how the brain can do these things. The **cerebral cortex** is the area of the brain that allows us to think. It sends information to other parts of the brain to be stored. The storage of this information is called memory. Scientists believe that memory is stored in many different parts of the brain.

Short-term memory

There are some things that you only need to remember for a short time. The brain only stores this information for as long as you need it. It is then forgotten. This is called short-term memory. An example is being able to remember a telephone number for long enough to dial the number.

Long-term memory

There are many things that you remember for days, months and years. Most people can remember their home

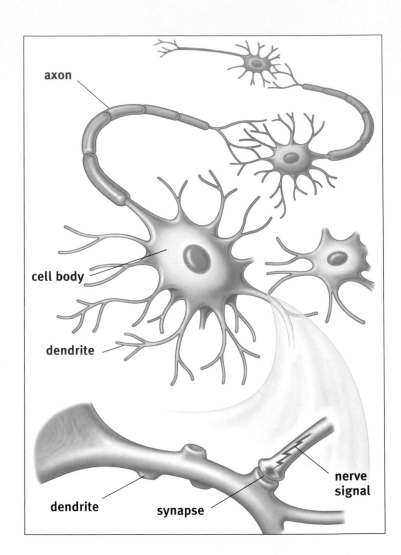

This diagram shows links between nerve cells.

address and telephone number. This is because they are stored as long-term memories.

Learning

We learn new things by repeating them over and over again. For example, when you read words, the eyes send signals to your brain. **Nerve cells** in the brain are made active. The brain then makes sense of what you have read. When you read the words again, the same nerve cells are made active. Connections are eventually made between these nerve cells. This means that if you read something many times, you begin to remember it.

When we learn things, new connections form in the brain.

Q&A

What is dyslexia?

Some people have a condition called dyslexia. These people are as intelligent as anybody else. However, they may find it difficult to read, write and spell. Dyslexia is often caused by short-term memory problems. Dyslexics can be taught special ways to help them deal with their problem. Many still do well at school.

Sleep and Dreams

Scientists do not know exactly why we sleep. They do know that we need sleep to survive. Going to sleep may be the body's way of saving energy. Also, while we sleep, the body can repair damage to the body caused during the day.

Sleep patterns

Our sleep is made up of five different stages. A typical night's sleep has several sleep cycles. During each cycle, we move from one sleep stage to the next.

Stages of sleep

Stage 1 sleep: The heartbeat and breathing slow down in the first few minutes of sleep. Muscles begin to relax.

Stage 2 sleep: At this stage, there are sudden bursts of brain activity.

Stage 3 sleep: This is deep sleep. The body temperature falls. **Brainwaves** become larger and slower.

Your brain is still working when you are asleep.

Stage 4 sleep: This is the deepest sleep stage. During this stage, the heartbeat and breathing slow even more. Brainwaves become even longer and slower.

REM sleep: The next stage is called rapid eye movement (REM) sleep. During this stage, our eyes move to and fro. They do this even while our eyelids are closed. In this stage, the heart and breathing speed up. Muscles begin to twitch. Brainwaves become faster and more irregular.

This diagram shows the typical sleep pattern for an adult.

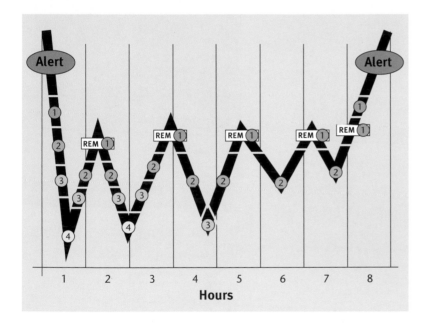

Dreams and REM sleep

We dream during REM sleep. We only remember our dreams if we wake up soon after the end of REM sleep. Scientists do not know why we dream. It may be a way of sorting out memories and learning.

Q&A

How much sleep do I need?

You need sleep for your body to rest and repair itself. Newborn babies need between 18 and 20 hours of sleep a day. Most adults need between six and eight hours each night. Children and teenagers need about ten or 11 hours sleep.

Feelings and Emotions

Every day we feel many different feelings and emotions. Sometimes we feel happy and loving. At other times we feel sad and scared. Your brain allows you to have these feelings. It also controls how you react to them.

Why we have feelings

Our feelings and emotions are linked to our senses and memory. For example, when you see a person coming towards you, your eyes send a signal to the brain. The brain works out what you have seen. If you know the person, the brain finds your memories of them. Good memories of the person will make you feel happy. If the memories are bad, you may feel sad or angry. Our senses of hearing, touch, smell and taste are linked to our memories in the same way.

All your feelings and emotions are controlled by the brain.

Fear

Fear is one of our most powerful emotions. When we feel scared, the brain helps the body prepare for action. The brain sends signals to our **adrenal glands.** The adrenal glands release a chemical called **adrenaline**. Adrenaline travels around the body in the blood. It prepares your body to fight or run away.

Effects of adrenaline

Adrenaline makes your heartbeat and breathing get faster. More oxygen and **nutrients** are pumped to your muscles. Your heart thumps. The muscles are prepared for action. You feel tense and shivery. Less blood flows to your skin. You become pale. Less blood flows to the **digestive system**. Your stomach feels empty and your mouth feels dry.

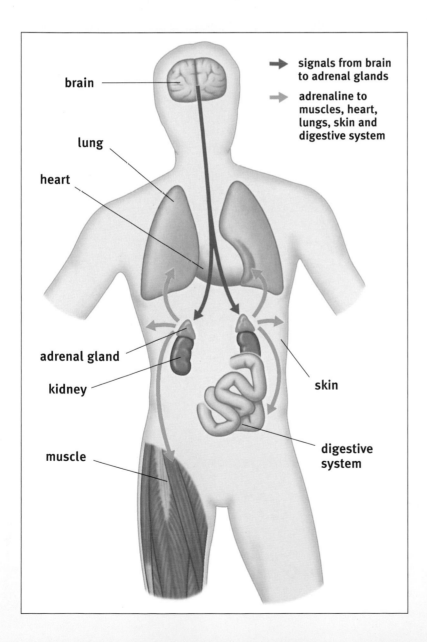

brain

lung

heart

adrenal gland

kidney

muscle

signals from brain to adrenal glands

adrenaline to muscles, heart, lungs, skin and digestive system

skin

digestive system

This diagram shows how the brain prepares the body when you are frightened.

Q&A

Why do I get 'butterflies' when I'm nervous?

Many people get 'butterflies' when they are anxious. This is because the brain thinks anxiety is fear. It signals to the adrenal glands. Adrenaline is pumped around the body. Less blood reaches the muscles of the digestive system. This causes the strange feeling in the stomach.

Brain Development

Our brains develop throughout our lives. Every new experience makes new connections between brain **cells**.

Babies

The shape of the brain is formed six months before a baby is born. Scientists think that babies can hear and recognize sounds in the womb. The brain is fully formed when the baby is born. A newborn baby's brain is about one-tenth of its adult weight. First, the baby begins to find out about its own body and the world around it. Then it starts to remember people and objects. The baby learns to communicate and control its movements. This happens because new connections are made between **nerve cells** in the brain.

One-year-olds

The brain grows quickly in the first year of life. A one-year-old brain is about two-thirds of its adult size. The baby has already learned many things. At no other time in our lives do we learn so much so quickly.

Babies can recognize their mother's face within a few days of being born.

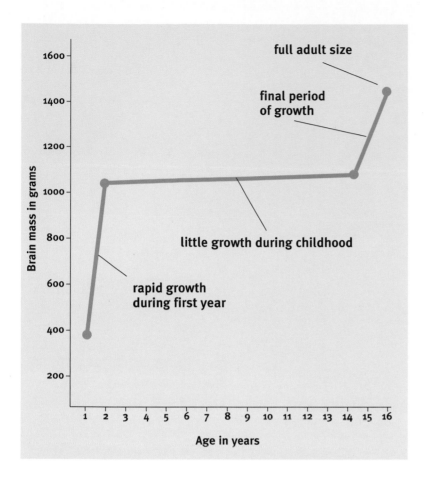

full adult size

final period
of growth

little growth during childhood

rapid growth
during first year

Brain mass in grams

Age in years

The brain grows quickest in the first year of life and
during the teenage years.

Childhood

The brain grows very little when we are children.
Most of the changes are inside the brain. They are
the result of learning and experience.

Teenage and adult years

The brain reaches full adult size between 14 and
16 years. Adults continue to learn and experience
new things every day. The brain develops new
connections and stores more memories. Many
adults can remember some things from when
they were three or four years old.

Q&A

Why are old people often forgetful?

Old people often forget
simple things such as
where they put something.
Yet they remember things
that happened to them as a
child really well. This
happens because
connections between nerve
cells in the brain break
down as we get older.
When a connection is
destroyed, the memory is
forgotten. Memories from
the distant past have
stronger connections.

When Things Go **Wrong**

Your brain will probably be healthy throughout your life. Sometimes, though, people have accidents or conditions that affect the brain. This can make life difficult for them.

Meningitis

The meninges are the thin layers between the brain and **skull**. Sometimes these get infected and become inflamed. This infection is called meningitis. Meningitis can be caused by a virus. This often seems like a bad dose of flu. Meningitis may also be caused by bacteria. This is more serious and can cause death. Antibiotics are used to fight this kind of meningitis.

Epilepsy

Some people have a condition called epilepsy. They have fits or **seizures**. During a seizure, they may hear sounds, see flashes of light and experience strange smells.

By putting electrodes on the skull, doctors can check electrical activity in the brain.

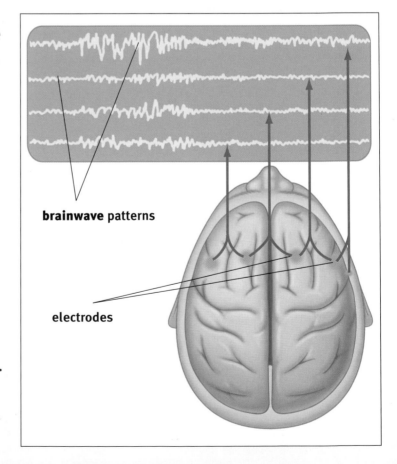

brainwave patterns

electrodes

Some people with epilepsy fall down during a seizure. They can't control their muscles and movements. Epilepsy is caused by occasional bursts of electrical activity in the brain. Some medicines can help to control it.

Concussion

Concussion is the most common brain injury. It is caused by a knock to the head. Anyone who has a blow to the head should be watched carefully. Concussion can cause headache, sleepiness, dizziness and loss of memory. Sometimes a blow to the head can cause more serious injuries to the brain.

Cerebral palsy

Cerebral palsy is caused by damage to the brain before birth. It can cause problems with balance, movement, speech, sight and hearing. Therapy can help people with cerebral palsy, but there is no cure.

The child on the right has cerebral palsy. The special wheelchair allows him to move around by himself.

Q&A

What is a headache?

Most headaches are the result of being tired, anxious or stressed. Headaches can also be caused by toothache, colds or eye strain. A rest or sleep will often make a person feel better. Sometimes medicine can help, too. Headaches are rarely caused by serious illness.

Glossary

adrenal glands — The parts of the body that produce adrenaline.

adrenaline — A hormone released when people feel frightened.

artery — One of the tubes that carry blood from your heart to the rest of your body.

autonomic nervous system — The parts of the brain and nerves that control and monitor your body automatically.

blood vessel — One of the tubes in the body through which your blood flows.

brainwave — An electrical signal in the brain.

cells — The tiny units from which all living things are made.

cerebellum — The part of the brain involved with movement and coordination.

cerebral cortex — The outer layers of the cerebrum.

cranial — To do with the skull.

digestive system — The parts of your body that break down food.

hypothalamus — The part of the brain involved in automatic responses, memories and emotions.

nerve — The part of the nervous system that carries signals or messages.

nerve cell — A single cell from a nerve or from inside the brain.

nutrients — Substances found in food that your body uses to keep healthy, fit and strong.

receptor — A nerve ending that detects some external stimulus, such as a touch or a smell.

reflex — An automatic reaction that does not go through the brain.

scanner — A machine that can search and examine things inside the body.

seizure — A sudden attack of illness.

sense organ — A structure that responds to the world around us, such as an eye, ear or nose.

skull — The bones of the head that protect the brain.

spinal canal — The space inside the spine that contains the spinal cord.

spinal cord — The bundle of nerve tissue inside the spinal canal.

spine — The backbone.

Further Information

Books

Body Science: Inside the Brain
by Rufus Bellamy (Franklin Watts, 2004)
Kingfisher Knowledge: Human Body
by Richard Walker (Kingfisher, 2006)
My Healthy Body: Brain and Senses
by Jen Green (Franklin Watts, 2003)
Our Bodies: The Brain and Nervous System
by Steve Parker (Wayland, 2003)
The Oxford Children's A to Z of the Human Body
by Bridget and Neil Ardley (Oxford University Press, 2003)
Usborne Internet-Linked Complete Book of the Human Body
by Anna Claybourne (Usborne Publishing, 2003)

Websites

www.innerbody.com (click on picture of nervous system)
www.bbc.co.uk/science/humanbody/body/factfiles/brain/brain.shtml
kidshealth.org/kid/htbw/brain.html

Index

Page numbers in **bold** refer to illustrations.